MARK OESTR[...]
& JOEL MAY[...]

A
PARENT'S
GUIDE

TO UNDERSTANDING

SEX & DATING

BEYOND THE BIRDS AND THE BEES

)) simply for parents

YouthMinistry.com/TOGETHER

A Parent's Guide to Understanding Sex & Dating
Beyond the Birds and the Bees

© 2013 Mark Oestreicher and Joel Mayward

group.com
simplyyouthministry.com

Credits
Authors: Mark Oestreicher and Joel Mayward
Executive Developer: Nadim Najm
Chief Creative Officer: Joani Schultz
Editor: Rob Cunningham
Cover Art and Production: Veronica Preston

ISBN 978-0-7644-8465-0

10 9 8 7 6 5 4 3 2   20 19 18 17 16 15 14 13

CONTENTS

CHAPTER 1: CREATING A FOUNDATION FOR SEXUALITY

The original title for this book was *A Parent's Guide to Sex*. We realized that title sounded a bit redundant—if you're a parent of a child, you've managed to figure out how to have sex at *least* once in your life. Maybe parents would pick it up thinking it was a how-to book for their sex lives now that they've got a bunch of kids in the house (hint: lock the door).

Unfortunately (or fortunately) for you, this is not that book.

First, a disclaimer: I (Joel) am not the parent of a teen. I do get *mistaken* for being a teenager all the time due to my natural youthful demeanor and inability to grow facial hair. But my eldest child is barely out of diapers, and as of this writing, I haven't even entered my 30s.

On the other hand, I (Marko) am way older than Joel. My half-century mark will be here in mere months, and I'm the dad of an almost-19-year-old, and an almost-15-year-old—one girl and one guy (which means I've *done it* at least twice!). But just because I've mostly weathered parenting one teenager and am in the midst of parenting another doesn't make me some sort of sex expert.

So why would we write a book on teen sexuality and dating intended for parents? And why should you even bother reading this?

Because we believe this stuff matters.

By "this stuff" we mean your teenager's well-being and future, particularly when it comes to their sexuality. Their future marriage and family and self-worth depend on it. We think you probably agree, which is why you've picked up this little book.

But "this stuff" is, frankly, difficult to talk about. It's hard and messy. Many parents and teens don't feel comfortable talking about sex openly, partly due to the intimate nature of the subject, and partly because they simply don't have an understanding of its complexity. It's pretty simple: Even if they think they *should* talk about it, they don't know *how* to talk about it and they don't *like* talking about it. So they don't.

The first time I (Joel) talked with my father about sexuality was in the Red Robin® located in my childhood stomping grounds of Federal Way, Washington. At the time, I was engaged to my soon-to-be wife and wanted a deeper friendship with my dad before I got married. In my naiveté, I broached the subject of sexuality. I figured, "We're two adult men now, so we could put childish ways behind us, right?" Wrong. He stiffened up, avoided eye contact, and spoke in a coded language, only referring to sex as "it" and "stuff." My dad is normally a very stoic man who isn't easily rattled, but this conversation had him squirming. I thought at one point that he'd actually spew his ranch-covered French fries all over the table from the nerves and anxiety.

That was the first and last time I talked with my dad about sex. I've still never broached the topic with my mom (and I don't plan to anytime soon).

When I (Marko) was a teenager, my parents found out that I'd been to a party where there was some fairly innocuous "making out" (and they were church kids!). Two days later, I found a book on my bed. It was called *Almost Twelve*. I was almost 15. Like Joel, the only *out-loud* conversation about sex I ever had with my dad was on the night before my wedding, and I remember it with nothing short of terror.

(Oddly enough, my parents—now in their late 70s—talk about sex all the time. It's simultaneously sweet, cute, and creepy.)

We're sharing these stories with you because we think we could have been saved a great deal of hurt and confusion in our lives if our (otherwise fantastic) parents simply would have talked with us about sex. We want to spare you and your teenager the same hurt and confusion. We think it's too important of a subject to *not* talk about.

We're hoping this little book feels more like a conversation than a how-to guide. Conversations about sexuality are important, but not in offensive or vague terms—we need to be able to have healthy, honest, theologically informed discussions about sex. It's been part of our story as human beings from the very beginning, and it plays a significant role in our identity formation. So we invite you to enter the conversation with open eyes and open ears. We'll strive to be candid without being crass, and authentic without over-sharing. (In other words, this won't be a book about our sex lives or filled with junior-high-level scatological humor, even though we have both been junior high pastors.)

Oh, one thing about us you should know: Both of us have been youth pastors for years (about 40 years between the two of us). In that context, we've talked with thousands of teenagers about the issues in this book, met with hundreds of parents, and read at least a few articles. So while our own parenting (particularly Marko's) will factor into what we have to say, we're mostly writing to you as youth workers who care deeply about your teenager, and about you.

Let's talk about "stuff."

A Theology of Sex — Back to the Beginning

A few years ago, I (Joel) went on a church mission trip to Mexico to build homes for impoverished families. I had done similar trips in high school, but this time we were building a real *house*. Doors, windows, roof, a concrete foundation—the works. Our first day was spent mixing concrete by hand and pouring it into a rectangle-shaped hole in the Mexican sand. Some of the men on our team literally spent hours making sure the edges of the hole were even and level, getting down with their faces in the dirt and making sure the concrete was smoothed and evenly distributed. Impatient and ignorant about architecture, I complained to one of the foremen that this was taking *forever*. He patiently explained that the foundation for the house made the framing and final construction possible. If we rushed ahead without doing the hard work of creating a level foundation—if we were only slightly off with our measurements—then the final house wouldn't be stable. It might take only days, or it might happen in a few years, but the results would be the same: The foundation would split. At best, the entire home would be slightly leaning; at worst, the house would collapse.

If we don't have a healthy foundation for our conversation on sex, then all of our ideas and thoughts and actions regarding sexuality will ultimately be skewed. They'll be slightly—or terribly—off-kilter. Our foundations have to be secure and right and true.

So allow us to get all theological on you and share some foundational thoughts from Scripture.

The first three chapters in the book of Genesis form a foundation for humanity's story. We first learn who God is. We learn about how the world was created and how humanity plays a part in that world. We learn about the relationship between God and human beings. We learn about how human beings broke that relationship. Genesis 1–2 gives us a picture of what life *should* be like, the Edenic paradise of living in peace and harmony with God and creation.

At the climax of the creation account, after God has created light and dark and earth and water and sky and vegetation and animals, something significant happens:

So God created human beings in his own image, in the image of God he created them; male and female he created them (Genesis 1:27 TNIV).

This passage is the first clear instance of poetry in the Bible. Poetry is used to express the inexpressible. This is important, because it means the author wants to highlight something, to draw our attention to an important truth: *Human beings are valuable to God.* All people—men, women, young, old, smart, not-so-smart, every race and ethnicity—every human being is made in the image of God. It's like we have the thumbprint of God in our lives, that we are a reflection of his beauty. The theological term for this is the *imago dei*, or the "image of God."

The implications are that if we treat human beings as any less than human beings, then we are not treating them how God created them to be. We are treating them as things, as objects, as tools. When we start treating people as objects and commodities to be used, then we are not valuing God's creation.

Treating human beings as less than human takes many forms that are directly connected to sexuality. There are obvious extremes, such as rape or the illegal sex slave trade. These horrible acts can only occur when human dignity and value are ignored, when the image of God is not acknowledged. As a culture, we all agree that these are forms of evil and depravity; they are outlawed, and justice is enforced against those who participate in such actions.

But there are more subtle ways we can turn people into objects, such as pornography, sexism, and lust. With pornography, a valuable human being with the image of God is distorted into a mere image used for selfish pleasure, or as a commodity to be sold in order to make money off people's lustful desires. With sexism, one gender dominates the other—usually male over female—degrading the other. Making sexist jokes or offensive comments about an entire gender removes the individual beauty of people.

The story of Genesis continues in chapter 2, describing how God created both man and woman. In verse 7, God forms the man from the dust and breathes the breath of life into his being. A second important truth occurs here: *We are created with both bodies and spirits.* We are more than just flesh and blood, but we also cannot ignore our bodily needs and desires. We'll talk more later on why this is so important, so file it away for now.

The man in the Garden of Eden turns out to be lonely, so God creates a woman out of the man's rib and brings her to the man. The man is obviously happy about this—he's been alone, and suddenly a naked woman appears. The author of Genesis describes something remarkable:

That is why a man leaves his father and mother and is united to his wife, and they become one flesh. Adam and his wife were both naked, and they felt no shame (Genesis 2:24-25 NIV).

This is the picture of the first marriage, the union between Adam and Eve in perfect unity with God and each other, all without sin. They could be both naked and unashamed. When we're naked, we're typically self-conscious, awkward, and exposed. Yet Adam and Eve could be completely vulnerable with each other and not feel a hint of disgrace. This is a holistic vulnerability, a sharing of their very being and identity with one another. It is perfect intimacy.

God's intention for human sexuality is quite clear here: *Sexuality was meant for marriage.* Marriage is the only healthy context where we as human beings can experience real sex, true sex, the kind that God desires for us. Anything else—premarital sex, adultery, hooking up, pornography, and so on—it's all just fake sex. It is choosing less than what God intended. This is the motivation behind the Christian mantra of "don't have sex before marriage." It's not because we are killjoys or prudes or stuck in outdated traditions. This is simply the best possible way to live out our sexuality.

Let us ask you a question: How sexual are you?

Ten percent? Fifty percent? Maybe closer to 90 percent? Depends on what you ate today?

Here's the answer: 100 percent. You are a sexual being. *Our sexuality and our identity are inherently intertwined.* God created us as male and female, set us in his creation, and said, "Be fruitful and multiply." Our human sexuality affects our bodies, our emotions, our desires, our dreams, and our fears. It's not that sex is the driving motivation behind all our actions and feelings. We're not getting all Freudian on you. Yet human sexuality is clearly wrapped up in the *imago dei*, and God created us as sexual beings, both by creating gender and the marriage covenant.

Having this theological foundation for our sexuality will set the tone for the rest of this little book. We'll be coming back to the foundation over and over again, because many of the sexual mistakes we make come from distorting or ignoring significant aspects of this foundation. We don't want your foundation to be tipsy or unstable, so come back to this section often to refresh your memory.

CHAPTER 2: MIXED MESSAGES— MYTHS ABOUT SEX

Myths From the Culture

If you take the time to listen to any number of pop songs playing on the radio or a teenager's iPod®, you'll notice that a majority of songs are about romance and love. Boyfriends, girlfriends, broken hearts, and the sex that gets intertwined in it all. If you listen to these songs long enough, you'll start to hear two distinct messages. On the one hand, there is a deep longing for fidelity and "the one," the person who will fulfill every longing and desire, the Romeo and Juliet story. On the other hand, lyrics speak of partying every night, hooking up with any number of partners, acting on impulse, and living for the moment. Which one is better: a committed relationship or a series of fun hookups and flings? If you look at our culture, you'd be hard-pressed to give a definitive answer.

A recent stat claims that more than 14,000 sexual references are shown on TV each year, and that the average person will view more than 100,000 of those references in his or her lifetime.[1] We'll be honest: That stat feels low to us. If culture is the water we swim in as a society, our 21st century American culture's view on sexuality could be summed up in one word: *confusion*. Swirling in the water are all sorts of mixed messages about love and sexuality. Many of these messages are considered normal and healthy even if they contradict one another or God's design for human sexuality.

We want to unpack a few common myths about sexuality that our culture is communicating to teenagers. Maybe you've believed some of these yourself; maybe you've never even considered them. Let us tell you: They're part of a teenager's world, and we need to have discernment in navigating the messages. Many of these myths are unpacked in greater detail in Lauren Winner's excellent book on sexuality, *Real Sex*.[2] Let's sift through the mixed messages together.

Cultural Myth #1: Sex is just an appetite.

We're told that sex is simply a craving we have as humans, similar to hunger or thirst. *I'm hungry, so I'm gonna eat this burger. I'm thirsty, so I need some water. I'm turned on, so I'm gonna have sex with my girlfriend.* Driven by impulse and desire, sexuality is just something we've gotta do as human beings.

One time in elementary school, my class (Joel) was let outside for recess. My friends and I usually played some form of tag or capture the flag. On this particular day, we ran outside to find a pile of feathers in the middle of the playground. It looked somewhat like a bird—but then we realized it was actually two birds. Were they fighting? Were they hurt? As we got closer, we came to the conclusion that any good fourth-grader would: They were definitely "doing it." The birds were getting it on, right in the middle of our playtime. After about 30 seconds, the birds separated and flew away. Tag would never be the same again.

Now, we're quite sure those birds were not thinking, "Does he only want me for my body, or does he really love me?" They probably weren't making future plans together or talking about what to name their kids. They weren't asking each other about the commitment level in the relationship; *they were birds*. But in our culture, we often reduce our sexuality to a biological function, don't we? We even have language for this: *a party animal, primal instinct, he or she is on the prowl*. In his book *Sex God*, Rob Bell makes this important observation:

> The assumption behind [this worldview] is that people are going to have sex because they can't

help themselves. This perspective is presented as freedom and honesty and just being who you are and doing what comes naturally, but it's built on the belief that certain things are inevitable. What it really teaches is that people cannot transcend the physical dimensions of their existence. It views people much like animals.[3]

This myth ignores one-half of the theological truth: *We are created with both bodies and spirits*. To declare that human beings can't help themselves when it comes to sex, that they are driven by their urges and desires, that they are just a cluster of hormones and bodily fluids ignores the spiritual dimension to our very beings. We are more than our impulses and hormones. Though these urges and desires are undoubtedly strong, our spiritual dimension empowers us both to experience something deeper than the physical act, and to express a fruit of the Spirit: self-control.

Cultural Myth #2: Everyone is having sex. Everyone.

When you watch movies and TV and hear stories about teenagers in the media, it's easy to conclude that absolutely everyone is having sex. While sexuality is certainly all around us, the claim that "everyone is doing it" simply isn't true.

In 2011, the National Center for Health Statistics reported a drop in teen sex. In that study over half of 15- to 17-year-olds (53 percent of males and 58 percent of females) reported never having had a sexual encounter with another person.[4] In October 2011, the Centers for Disease Control and Prevention also reported news along similar lines: Less than half of youth ages 15-19 (42 percent of unmarried males and 43 percent of unmarried females) report having had intercourse. That's all the way to age 19, which includes post-high school students in their first years of college. The CDC report also pointed out that the main reasoning for never having had sex was "against religion or morals" (28 percent for females, 27 percent for males), with "don't want to get pregnant" as a significant second reason.[5]

Also interesting, the CDC data "show clear patterns of sexual experience among teenagers by family and parental characteristics. For both male and female teenagers, a significantly smaller percentage were sexually experienced if:

- They lived with both parents when they were aged 14

- Their mothers had their first birth at age 20 or over

- The teenager's mother was a college graduate

- The teenager lived with both of her/his parents [at the time of the survey]."[6]

Here's what this tells us: You, as the parent, have significant influence in your teenager's life regarding sexual choices. Are a lot of teenagers having sex in our culture? Sure. But a significant number are choosing to abstain, poking a large hole in this cultural myth. The statistics reveal that it is absolutely possible for a teenager to not have sex. The idea that teen intercourse is inevitable is patently false. It also reveals that when parents are present and engaged with their teen, they can guide their son or daughter in making wise sexual decisions.

Cultural Myth #3: As long as you don't go "all the way," sex is no big deal.

This myth is connected to the first myth, that sex is just an appetite. The thinking is, "As long as I don't actually have actual intercourse, it's OK." Oral sex, masturbation, pornography, making out with some random person at a party are all fine, as long as we don't have the possibility of getting pregnant. Many younger teenagers, in their desire to experiment with their newfound sexuality, adopt this view. Religious teenagers will also adopt this mindset as a rationalization for sexual behavior.

Remember Adam and Eve? They were "naked and unashamed," meaning that they were entirely vulnerable before each other. This vulnerability is holistic: bodies, emotions, spirits, values. Sex connects two people in a way that is similar to the relationship the members of the Trinity have with one another. It was intended to be a picture of that union. Reducing sex to a series of brief physical encounters ignores a huge component of what God intended sex to be. Tim Keller writes about sexuality's holistic nature in *The Meaning of Marriage*:

> To call marriage "one flesh," then, means that sex is understood as both a sign of that personal, legal union and a means to accomplish it. The Bible says don't unite with someone physically unless you are also willing to unite with the person emotionally, personally, socially, economically, and legally. Don't become physically naked and vulnerable to the other person without becoming vulnerable in every other way, because you have given up your freedom and bound yourself in marriage.[7]

The more physical one becomes with another person, the more connected they become in every other way. This is why when two people have had sex together and then break up, it can be far more emotionally devastating. They have given themselves to each other beyond the physical, often without even realizing it. It felt great when they were together, but now there is a bond that they never expected to be there.

There are no flippant sexual encounters. Remember, we are 100 percent sexual beings, meaning that our sexuality is intertwined with our identity, affecting every other facet of our life and being. It's more than just intercourse; it's the intertwining of two persons. Reducing sexual encounters to these brief physical releases is just that: a reduction. It's less than God intended for us.

Ask yourself: Have I believed any of these myths? What about my teenager? Have an honest conversation about it, and strive to seek the truth.

Myths From the Church

I (Joel) love movies. You could call me an amateur film expert. (You don't have to, but I'd sure appreciate it!) As I was recently scanning the Internet for upcoming films, an independent documentary caught my eye: *Jesus, Don't Let Me Die Before I've Had Sex*. This is from the filmmaker, Matt Barber:

> As a young Christian, I was led to believe that sex held a magical power that would transform me into a man and heal all of my insecurities—even more so if I remained pure before marriage. Imagine my surprise after my wedding night when I realized, "I feel like the same person."
>
> *Jesus, Don't Let Me Die Before I've Had Sex* will be a feature-length documentary examining the teachings of the evangelical church on sex and exploring the undercurrent of idealism that leaves many lay members feeling frustrated and confused. The movie will paint a picture of what is taught explicitly and implicitly by showing how churchgoers implement those teachings—through anecdotes of first kisses, chastity rallies, and secret obsessions.[8]

I certainly have prayed that prayer before. As a teenager, the coming of the Savior of the world felt secondary to my own desire to have my sexual desires fulfilled. In essence, my desire for sex trumped my desire for Jesus. Barber's film reveals the underlying truth: The church hasn't been the greatest at explaining the truth about sex. In fact, we have just as many myths as the surrounding culture. Ours are just harder to discern and redeem, because they are often masked under the veneer of holiness and purity. They are our hidden insecurities and ignorance about sexuality dressed up in spiritual language.

As we explore these myths together, take stock of your own reactions and beliefs. *What do you really believe about sexuality?* (Again, many of these myths are unpacked in Lauren Winner's fantastic book, *Real Sex*, which you should probably go purchase and read as soon as you're done with this book.)

Church Myth #1: Sex and bodies are dirty.

It was my wedding night (Joel). My wife and I entered our bedroom—*our* bedroom—and were nervously excited about consummating our new marriage. We were both virgins, both raised in the church, both eager to experience the fullness of our sexuality. It was the moment I had been waiting for—Jesus could surely come back after tonight's activities.

Imagine my surprise when it turned out that sex was…
well…uncomfortable. Difficult. Awkward. I thought it was
supposed to feel amazing, like a euphoria that would
be akin to physical transcendence. Instead, it felt weird.
Was this what it was supposed to be like? Were we doing
something wrong? Was there something wrong with me?

As my wife and I talked about it over our honeymoon,
we realized that we both had similar expectations for
our wedding night. This experience was *supposed* to be
incredible. After all, that's what we had heard at all the
abstinence talks and purity rallies we had participated in
over the years.

We felt like we had believed a lie.

The church had sent a mixed message: *Sex is wrong,
sex is evil, sex is disgusting and perverted—so save it for
marriage*. Many of the teenagers we disciple who are raised
in the church awkwardly squirm when the subject of sex
is brought up. It's a taboo idea, something that is "dirty" or
"bad."

What happens if we tell teenagers that having sexual
feelings is inherently wrong and sinful? What happens if

Christian parents don't talk with their children about sex because it's just something that Christians don't talk about? What happens if a student is scolded or shamed for asking a pastor questions about sex? What happens when a junior high girl begins having her period, or a junior high guy experiences a nocturnal emission? What messages are being picked up?

The treatment of bodies as inherently sinful is actually common throughout Christian history; we would call this unbiblical thinking *Gnosticism*. Part of Gnosticism says that all created matter—including the human body—is bad, particularly sexual desire. The Gnostics would strive to repress or ignore all bodily desires, focusing on the spiritual world and their spiritual nature. To escape the body was essential to spiritual maturity.

If the cultural myth ignores our spirituality and claims we are only bodies, then this church myth emphasizes the spiritual to the detriment of the physical. Lauren Winner unpacks the basics for Christian sexual ethics in terms of the created body:

> But the starting point is this: God created us with bodies; God Himself incarnated in a human body; Jesus was raised again from the dead with a

body; and one day we too will be resurrected with our bodies. That is the beginning of any Christian ethic—any moral theology—of how human beings in bodies interact with other bodies.[9]

Yes, the inherent goodness of our bodies was distorted and perverted with the invasion of sin into human history. But God's thumbprint of the *imago dei* still resides within our bodies. There is no divorce of the physical and spiritual in Scripture; our bodies and sexuality are deeply valuable to God, and thus should be valuable to us.

Instead of viewing the human body as something to overcome or tolerate, we must first view our bodies as gifts from God and capable of bringing him glory. Parents, don't get subtly caught up in a form of Gnosticism. If all your conversations about sex and bodies are conducted with a negative tone, teenagers will hear the message loud and clear. Be willing to talk with them about their developing bodies in healthy and positive ways.

Church Myth #2: Sex outside of marriage is guaranteed to make you feel terrible.

In many Christian circles, conversations around premarital sex will often lead to the theme of guilt. *If I sleep with my boyfriend/girlfriend, I'll be racked with shame. I'll wake up the next morning feeling horrible and alone. I will have ruined God's gift of sexuality forever.*

Sure, that's sometimes true, but it isn't always. Sometimes after committing a sinful act—sexual or not—we can feel fantastic! Remember, sex can be pleasurable and fun; it was designed to be. Thus, even casual "hookup" sex can feel pretty great and not necessarily leave the participants feeling guilty or shameful, even though the theological reality is that no hookup is ever truly "casual." This is especially true when two people are unmarried but in a committed relationship, through cohabitation and/or longevity. "We're in love, we know that we want to spend our lives together—at least for now—so why not have sex?"

Perhaps the church has missed something here, choosing to lay extensive guilt trips upon hormonal teenagers in the hope that they'll want to avoid premarital sex. What happens, then, if a young person does have a sexual encounter—intercourse or otherwise—and *doesn't* feel guilty afterward? In that moment, what will they trust: the strong feelings and urges that feel genuinely amazing, or the apparently erroneous message the church has been feeding them? Lauren Winner points out the theology behind this false reasoning:

This is how sin works: it whispers to us about the goodness of something not good. It makes distortions feel good. It tells us we'd be better off with pleasure in hell than sanctification in heaven. In insisting that premarital sex will make you feel bad, the church is misstating the nature of sin and the nature of our fallen hearts. The plain, sad fact is that we do not always feel bad after we do something wrong. To acknowledge that premarital sex—or any other sinful act—might *feel* good is not to say that premarital sex *is* good.[10]

Parents can perpetuate the guilty feelings by talking about sex in hushed tones (see Church Myth #1) or making it abundantly clear that teenagers are never, *ever* allowed to mess this one up. As parents, we may try to protect our children by pointing out the dangers of premarital sex, but hiding them from the fact that sex is genuinely pleasurable will not prepare them for the moments of temptation. If the only message a teen has heard is "you'll feel guilty," they'll gladly toss that message out if experience tells them otherwise.

Church Myth #3: Singleness is Plan B.

There are plenty of 20-somethings feeling pressured by people in the church—and their own hormones and desires—to get married and start a family. We've noticed there's a confusing message in the Christian subculture: When you're young and in junior high or high school, people will tell you: "Don't date, don't have sex, be cautious, just don't go there." And as soon as they enter college, the message changes: "When are you getting married? Any new prospects?" If you glance at the number of Christian books, seminars, conferences, websites, and ministries specially designated for marriage, you might think that marriages are the top priority of the church.

The problem? While marriage is clearly a God-given gift, it is never an excuse to create a hierarchy between married and single. Single people are not second-class citizens in the kingdom of God. Some fairly important people in Scripture were single; the Apostle Paul and Jesus Christ come to mind. In fact, Paul calls singleness a "gift" in 1 Corinthians 7:7. I (Joel) used to think this "gift" meant that a person didn't have a desire for marriage or sex, but I've changed my view on this. Tim Keller unpacks the gift of singleness in *The Meaning of Marriage*:

> The "gift-ness" of being single for Paul lay in the freedom it gave him to concentrate on ministry in ways that a married man could not….Consider, then, that the "single calling" Paul speaks of is

neither a condition without any struggle nor on the other hand an experience of misery. It is fruitfulness in life and ministry *through* the single state.[11]

If you're a single parent, you are not less loved or valued in God's eyes. Neither are your unmarried teenage children. Young people need to know that while marriage is a gift from God, following Jesus is not ultimately determined by one's relationship status.

CHAPTER 3: DUDES AND CHICKS— GENDER-SPECIFIC SEXUAL ISSUES

While the myths in Chapter Two affect both teenage guys and girls alike, there are some gender-specific issues that affect teenagers in unique ways. We're convinced that nearly all sexuality issues for both genders stem from a foundational misunderstanding: missing the *imago dei*. But that misunderstanding tends to be (admittedly, these are generalizations) the opposite in girls and guys.

Teenage Guys

Teenage guys tend to miss the *imago dei* in others. The image of God in human beings makes us beautiful and unique masterpieces. Guys tend to ignore this divine thumbprint and replace it with a utilitarian objectification of others. In other words, people stop being subjects and become objects. The evidence of this view is revealed in prevalent lust that occurs in teenage guys. This includes, but is not limited to, visually "checking out" girls walking by, locker room talk about their sexual feats, raunchy movies and TV shows, viewing pornography, and internal sexual fantasizing.

In *Wired for Intimacy: How Pornography Hijacks the Male Brain*, author William Struthers writes this:

> As men fall deeper into the mental habit of fixating on these images, the exposure to them creates neural pathways. Like a path is created in the woods with each successive hiker, so do the neural paths set the course for the next time an erotic image is viewed. Over time these neural paths become wider as they are repeatedly traveled with each exposure to pornography. They become the automatic pathway through which interactions with women are routed. The neural circuitry anchors this process solidly in the brain. With each lingering stare, pornography deepens a Grand Canyon-like gorge in the brain through which images of women are destined to flow. This extends to women that they have not seen naked or engaging in sexual acts as well. *All women become potential porn stars in the minds of these men. They have unknowingly created a neurological circuit that*

imprisons their ability to see women right as created in God's image (emphasis ours).[12]

This is why pornography and lust are so destructive for young men. Sexuality becomes a consumerist pursuit, treating women as visual objects used for the personal pleasure in a given moment. It's not that women don't also have struggles with pornography and lust (they do), but the root issue here is theological—young men have a wrong view of the humanity around them, which in turn affects their view of themselves.

Guys need to have accountability for how they view others. Parents can provide that accountability if they've taken the time to create a culture of honesty within the family (more on that in just a moment). Guys need to be reminded that how they view others is directly connected to how well their hearts are aligned with Christ. Jesus tells us in the Sermon on the Mount, *"But I say to you that everyone who looks at a woman with lustful intent has already committed adultery with her **in his heart** (Matthew 5:28 ESV*, emphasis added*)."* This is a heart issue, not just a behavior issue. The best accountability addresses issues of the heart, not just chiding for poor behavior or offering a pat on the back after a weekly confession of sin.

Teenage Girls

Teenage girls tend to miss the *imago dei* in themselves. They lose sight of the divine thumbprint in their own souls, finding self-worth and value in their sexuality. It is substituting the image of God for one's body image. Our media culture perpetuates this myth by constantly bombarding teenage girls with false images and portrayals of femininity. "True women," these voices say, "are thin and tall and blemish-free and have perfect eyelashes and perfect breasts and perfect hips and perfect hair and dozens of attractive men fawning over them."

This kind of pressure leads to young women questioning their self-worth. It can lead to eating disorders, dramatic changes in wardrobe and fashion, and comparison games with other teenage girls around them. The insecurity and longing to be desired can become quite overwhelming for a young woman. A recent phenomenon among tween girls has been the posting of videos to YouTube® asking the question "Am I ugly?" The comments and responses are, sadly, often derogatory and demeaning. Notice the question: It's not "Am I beautiful?" or "Am I a good person?" It's entirely negative and based on external physical features. These girls are longing for someone to answer that question: *No, you're not ugly. You're beautiful and valuable and uniquely wonderful.*

As parents, we can affirm our daughters in their character and beauty beyond their external features. Their value is found in the unique beauty of how God has created them. Psalm 139 reminds us that we're knit and formed together by God in his divine love. Tell them often that they're beautiful without pretense or prompting.

For both guys and girls, whether they are missing the *imago dei* in others or themselves, they're not living into the way of true humanity. Remind them often how unique and wonderful they are as creations of God, particularly in their sexuality. Point out the *imago dei* whenever you see it, and look for it often.

CHAPTER 4: TALKING WITH YOUR TEENAGER—CREATING A CULTURE OF HONESTY

Most teenagers are not thrilled about talking with their parents about sexuality and dating. If we're honest, most parents are equally apprehensive about discussing it with their sons and daughters. More often than not, the parents we've encountered take one of three approaches to talking about sex:

1. **They don't.** *Ever.* It's a taboo subject in the home and comes up as often as quantum physics or the migratory patterns of arctic waterfowl. Or maybe less often than that.

2. **The sex talk.** Puberty happens. When it does, these parents talk about sex one time with their kids. *One.* Singular. Uno. It's essentially an awkward anatomy lesson about what parts fit where.

3. **The reluctant-yet-explosive reaction.** There's talk about sex only when the parents are angry about their teenager's decisions regarding sexuality. The tone is entirely negative and occurs after reaching a dramatic climax. (That innuendo was unavoidable, right?)

We'd like to propose an alternative to these three common approaches: Create a culture of honesty with your teenager.

The word *honesty* is related to *honor*, and goes far beyond "telling the truth." It encompasses morality, integrity, and a healthy respect toward the subject and person. It's having a relational vibe that says, "Yeah, we can talk about this. I know that I won't be judged or rejected, and that I'll learn and grow from this conversation." And it *is* a conversation, a dialogue between two (or three) human beings. This isn't about learning how to talk *at* your teen, but *with* your teen about sexuality and dating. There are a few ways to foster this sort of relational ethos with your teenager:

Listen and Learn

Fostering a culture of honesty is entirely built upon trust. Teens are asking, "Can I trust my parent(s) with this decision, question, or feeling about sex and dating?" If they don't trust that you will respond with grace, understanding, and compassionate wisdom, then the conversations surrounding sexuality—and, really, *anything*—will feel stilted and shallow.

While some things about teenage romance, dating, and sexuality haven't changed since you were a teenager, a dramatic number of these things have completely changed. I (Joel) am barely a decade out of my own teenage experience, and I am still flabbergasted at how *different* the culture has become in such a short period of time. We'll give you a brief history of dating and romance later in this book, but we can agree now that culture has been morphing at an ever-increasing speed, including our expectations and ideas about sexuality and dating.

You can still empathize with your teenager's experience without projecting your own experience upon theirs. Listen to their stories. *Really* listen. Become a student of youth culture. Know what messages the media are sending your teen through television, film, music, and the Internet. This will require a posture of humility and appreciation.

Share Your Story

Building trust requires vulnerability and fidelity on your part. Being vulnerable requires sharing your own story about sexuality and dating. Even if your story is filled with mistakes and heartache, share honestly about your first dating experience and your sexual journey. You don't have to be explicit or graphic, but you can humbly offer your experience. Empathize with their struggles, too. If you know what it's like to have your heart broken after a dating relationship falls apart, share that. Talk about the consequences of your own decisions—good, bad, and ugly. Teenagers need to hear how others' experiences went down and where choices ultimately led.

Hear us: This doesn't mean that you project your story on your teen's story. Remember that he or she is a unique individual created with the *imago dei*. God is shaping their story in unique and beautiful ways. Share in order to empathize and normalize their experience, recognizing that your stories will be—and should be—different.

Initiate and Engage

In both of our youth ministries, we have a mantra for our volunteer leaders regarding engaging teenagers:

We get to be awkward so they don't have to.

As youth workers, we must choose to engage with students without waiting for them to approach us on the subject. This doesn't mean diving into the deep end of the conversational pool right away. ("Hey, how was your day? Have any sexual experiences?") It simply means choosing to get over the social insecurities we have and initiating conversations with our teens.

A huge piece of initiating and engaging is learning how to ask good questions. Most teenagers aren't going to offer a long commentary of their thoughts on sexuality on their own. Parents need to ask, but not with a demanding tone. This is a healthy curiosity and interest, not an interrogation. Ask open questions that go beyond a simple "yes" or "no" answer.

When you watch a movie or TV show together, notice the messages being sent about sexuality and romance. Point them out casually afterward, and ask your teen if they noticed or thought about them. When a school dance is coming up and your teenager's friends are talking about dates and romance, ask what your son or daughter is thinking and feeling about the whole thing. Look for opportunities to make teachable moments and conversation starters out of everyday life circumstances, often without a neatly concrete platitude from you.

What Not to Do in Five Easy Steps

Feel like ruining your teenager's life? Want to remove any trust you've built and continue to perpetuate myths about sexuality and dating? Then follow these five easy steps to sexual destruction!

1.   When your son or daughter hits puberty, make plenty of jokes and sarcastic comments about their changing bodies. That way, they'll develop a wonderful sense of insecurity and self-loathing.

2.   Let your teen have completely free reign of the Internet. Don't install any of those annoying filters, and certainly don't set any boundaries about Internet usage. Hey, just give them a laptop when they're 10 years old. That way they'll be able to develop a pornography addiction *before* they become a teenager.

3.   Never share your expectations for romance or dating. Just let your teenager figure it out on their own—and then explode on them if they haven't met your expectations. (More on dating expectations later in the book!)

4.   When your teen approaches you with questions, concerns, or stories about sex and dating, look at

them like they're totally crazy. Maybe laugh at them or get really freaked out. This will prevent any more of those annoying conversations.

5. If your teenager is dating someone, don't get to know that person. Avoid interaction at all costs, and try to make them feel uncomfortable being in your home. Make it clear that romance needs to happen *outside* of the home, like in the backseat of a car.

CHAPTER 5: GREAT EXPECTATIONS— UNDERSTANDING BOUNDARIES IN DATING

A History Lesson on Dating

What guidance can parents give their teens in the realm of dating? To answer that question, we'd like to remind you of some historical realities of dating and romance in Western culture.

Way back in the day—as in, hundreds of years ago, and well into the 18th and 19th centuries in America—marriages were usually arranged by families. The big motivations for marriage were societal and financial—two family units wanted to form a partnership that would benefit both families. So they had their kids get married. Marriages had huge family involvement, and romance usually had nothing to do with it.

Something changed in the 19th century: People started to marry for romantic love. (Think Jane Austen novels.)

A system of courtship, or "calling," was formed. A man "called" on a young woman by coming over to her home and hanging out together with the family. Romance was still predominantly in a family context, but now it was more of an invitation for a man to pursue a woman rather than an arrangement ordained for them.

With the onset of youth culture thanks to the acceptance of the high school in the middle of the 20th century, the concept of "dating" appeared. Tim Keller writes in *The Meaning of Marriage*:

> Now the young man did not so much come in but instead took the woman out to places of entertainment to get to know her. As dating spread throughout society, it not only individualized the whole process, removing the couple from the family context, but it also changed the focus of romance from friendship and character assessment to spending money, being seen, and having fun. [13]

Dating has been the predominant form of romance leading to marriage in American culture, though there have been some conservative groups that propose a "going back to courtship" model of romance.

Beyond dating, a new social change has occurred in only the last few years in Western culture: the "hookup." A 2004 *New York Times Magazine* article reported how teenagers found dating to be too much work, requiring the give-and-take of communication and learning to have a committed relationship with another person.[14] Rather than having to go through the difficult process of developing a relationship with another person, the hookup emerged. A hookup is a simple sexual encounter without the condition of conducting an actual relationship. Maybe you start dating the person you just had sex with. Maybe you don't. Either option is considered fine.

With the emergence of the hookup culture, we are currently living in a society where sexual expression and marriage are completely separated. There are no clear and normative ways for young people to pursue marriage. We regularly have conversations with teenagers and young adults who literally have no idea how to get from singleness to marriage in a healthy way. They're struggling to figure out a "Christian" way to date, often with messy and confusing results.

In the midst of this, the average age for marriage has progressively increased over the past century, and skyrocketed in the past few decades. An article from *The Atlantic* explores the changing dynamic of marriage in America:

> In 1960, 72% of all adults over 18 were married. By 2010, the number fell to 51%. You can fault the increase in divorces that peaked in the 1970s. Or you could just blame the twentysomethings. The share of married adults 18-29 plunged from 59% in 1960 to 20% in 2010.[15]

The U.S. Census Bureau states that the average age for first-time brides and grooms is the highest it's ever been: 26.5 years old for brides and 28.7 for grooms (these numbers are changing *very* quickly, so it's important to note that we're quoting 2009 census data for the U.S. only).[16] On the other end of things, the average age of puberty has actually lowered over the past century, with the average for girls hovering around 10.5 years old, and 12 in boys.

Christian parents: See why "just wait until marriage" simply doesn't work? We're not asking the same discipline of teenagers that we were even 20 years ago. Where a teen alive in biblical times might actually find themselves married *before* the onset of puberty, we're asking 21st-century young people to put sexual intercourse on hold for *15 or more years.* That kind of abstinence is totally possible, but it's also not something to be taken lightly. (More on this in the next section.)

A few final thoughts on this history lesson: First, there isn't a "biblical" way to date (contrary to what some of the courtship proponents might want you to believe). The modern concept of dating simply didn't exist when the Bible was written. This is why any book, seminar, or curriculum offering the "biblical" way to date—in other words, the only correct way—raises red flags for us. Of course there are biblical principles regarding sexuality, humanity, and God's desires about marriage. That's why having a good theological foundation about sexuality is so important—you can build a healthy and godly set of expectations for dating based on truths from the Bible about how God designed human sexuality.

Why Saying "Just Wait" Isn't Enough

From purity banquets to sex-and-dating teaching series in youth groups, the message of "just wait until marriage" is everywhere in the church world. I (Joel) remember going through a purity ceremony in my Baptist youth group, where I received my own purity ring to place on my left hand, supposedly until the day I got married. Both the ring and the ceremony were uncomfortable. Something just didn't fit. I didn't understand *why*. Why wait? If two people are truly in love, why delay the expression of that love? Why did this seem to be such a big deal in the Christian subculture? If "just wait" is the message, then what's the reasoning behind it? (By the way, some research and *lots and lots* of anecdotal observations seem to reveal that purity pledges don't actually make a significant difference in sexual behavior. They *might* postpone intercourse a bit, but there's some indication that they also might *increase* other sexual experiences.)

We think our language about "just wait" needs to change. The reality is that most folks sharing the message don't know why they're sharing it. It's just the Christian thing to say, right? But that message simply doesn't work in the heat of the moment. While the statistics cited earlier reveal that less than half of teenagers are engaged in sexual intercourse, a recent study conducted by The National Campaign to Prevent Teen and Unplanned Pregnancy revealed that 88 percent of unmarried young adults (ages 18-29) are having sex. Of those surveyed who self-identified as "evangelical," 80 percent said they have had sex.[17] Even if the purity banquets worked at age 16, they simply aren't very convincing at age 26.

Instead of sharing the negative message of "don't have sex or else you're sinning," the message needs to become "chastity is a discipline of the gospel life."

Spiritual disciplines are actions that we do in order to orient our heart, soul, mind, and strength in the ways of Jesus and his gospel. This isn't salvation by works; it's a disciplined response to align our thoughts, emotions, and actions within the will of God. Chastity is one of these spiritual disciplines. Lauren Winner writes, "It is not the mere absence of sex but an active conforming of one's body to the arc of the gospel."[18] Chastity is not only for single people prior to marriage; it encompasses both abstinence before marriage and fidelity within marriage.

> Here the discipline of sex is twofold. Fidelity is a discipline; just as most single people want to have sex, period, so married people (even really happily married people) find themselves wanting to have sex with someone other than their spouse. And restraining those impulses is itself a discipline. (Indeed, it is worth pointing out that practicing chastity before you are married trains you well for chastity after you are married; it stands to reason that those who are promiscuous before marriage

may be more likely to cheat on their spouses once married.)[19]

Talking about chastity in this way changes it from a frustrating religious rule to a life-giving spiritual practice. It recognizes that *this is really difficult*, that God is asking us to do something that goes against both our cultural expectations and our inner impulses. Disciplines are not meant to be easy, but they are meant to make us better people and provide us a more full life. Chastity is, in essence, a sexual form of fasting. It is not allowing our impulses and desires—good, God-given ones, like hunger, thirst, and sexual desire—to ultimately define our actions and lifestyle. The goal of chastity is to be more like Jesus, to tap into the kingdom life that he has revealed to us. Practicing chastity is essential because it is a reflection of the good news that Jesus is faithful to us.

Full disclosure: I (Marko) didn't quite wait. And "didn't quite wait" really means that I wasn't a virgin when I got married. There was only one other girl, one other time, prior to my wife. But I, like so many committed Christian teenagers and young adults (which I was), misstepped. However, I (Joel) *did* wait. My wife is the only woman I have ever had sexual intercourse with. I didn't even kiss a girl until age

18. I didn't tell my wife "I love you" until the next words out of my mouth were "will you marry me?" because I didn't want to cheapen that overused expression of affection. That was really hard, because I definitely loved her long before I popped the question. I'm nothing special, and I certainly had my own struggles with lust and sexual sin. But I waited, and it was totally worth it. I share this because both you and your teenager need to hear that *it is possible to wait*. It's not easy, but it can be done.

Creating Healthy Expectations for Dating

With a theological foundation for sexuality, a general understanding of the history and culture of dating, and the message of chastity as a spiritual discipline, what expectations should parents have for their teenagers and dating?

Here's the challenging part: We can't answer that question for you.

Seriously. We can't. Every family system and situation is unique, and we can't give you a formulaic answer for what expectations to have. What we can give you is a framework for creating healthy and godly expectations for sex and dating. This is a conversation you need to invite your teenager to be a part of as you create these expectations, by the way. Teenagers won't be (or shouldn't be) setting the final expectations or boundaries for themselves, but they do need to have a sense of ownership and a clear reasoning behind the expectations set before them, or they will never live into them. They may not agree with all the expectations, but they certainly need to have a clear understanding of them.

This framework is a series of five questions:

- **What does the Bible say about sexuality?** This is the theological foundation about sexuality that includes much of what was previously mentioned in this book. What does Scripture really say about sex? Read some key passages about sexuality with your teenager (such as Genesis 1–2, Song of Solomon, Matthew 5:27-30, 1 Corinthians 6–7).

- **What are the cultural and contextual realities about dating and romance?** This is the current sexuality and dating "climate" of your own context. What school does your teenager attend? What are the cultural norms and expectations in your neighborhood? your church? your family? This doesn't mean that your context will be the ultimate defining factor, but it does need to be recognized and addressed by you and your teen. A home-schooled teenage guy with no siblings living with both his parents will have a different context than a teenage girl with six siblings and divorced parents attending a large public school.

- **What are the unique competencies of my teenager?** Every teenager is different and matures at a different rate. What is the maturity level of your teen, and how do you measure "maturity"? How responsible are they? How well do they understand a biblical foundation for sexuality? Some teens may be ready to date at age 16; some may not. Some may need an early curfew; some may be fine with no curfew. The onset of puberty, birth order, gender, and personality are all important factors in evaluating what your teenager is capable of handling.

- **What are the unique temptations of my teenager?** What are the sexual struggles, present and potential, of your teen? Remember the sexual mistakes of teenage guys and girls—missing the *imago dei* in others and themselves, respectively. A teenage girl who hits puberty earlier than her peers will have temptations that will be far different from the teenage guy who's a late bloomer.

- **What boundaries does my teenager need?** This is the final question that can finally be answered after the previous four have been addressed. It's a question that needs to have ownership from both parent and teen; there needs to be a conversation about what these boundaries are and why they exist. Boundaries may address Internet, cell phone, and media use; curfews; age to begin dating; where/when time is spent with a boyfriend/girlfriend; clothing and modesty; and participation in activities such as dances, banquets, or parties.

Creating clear boundaries happens best once a culture of honesty has been created in your family. To simply create an arbitrary set of rules for your teenager will likely lead to frustration at best and rebellion at worst. However, not having any boundaries also will get your teenager into hot water. They need you as a parent to give them clear guidelines and limits, and to hold them accountable.

Beyond boundaries, create a set of "dating criteria" with your teen. What are the character traits that need to be present in the person he or she chooses to date? These traits and values need to go beyond "he's nice" or "she's hot." Search through Scripture and come up with a framework for the kind of person that is worth marrying, and thus worth dating. This isn't about becoming legalistic or judgmental toward others. It's simply being intentional about one of the most important decisions in your teen's life—finding a person they could potentially marry.

You don't have to do navigate this alone; find two or three other parents of teenagers that you respect and trust, and ask them about the boundaries and expectations they've created in their family. You might find some great practical wisdom—or learn how you *don't* want to parent your teenager.

CHAPTER 6: SPECIFIC ISSUES IN SEX AND DATING

This might be the section of the book you looked at first. Because there are so many different cultural issues involving teenagers, sex, and dating, it's difficult to create an exhaustive list! However, we've done our best to offer bits of wisdom and insight into a variety of issues of sex and dating in the world of today's teenager.

Masturbation

This might be the one section of this little book where it's the most difficult to avoid euphemisms (that would likely make dads chuckle and get moms annoyed). This is a touchy subject! (See what we mean?)

Masturbation is one of those subjects that Christians (both churches and Christian parents) have done a horrible job of addressing. We mostly avoid talking about it at all, ever. And when we do (typically in churches, because so few parents ever talk about this with their kids), it's usually in a way that leads to guilt and condemnation, but isn't all that helpful.

The reality is this: All teenage guys masturbate (maybe there's a one-in-a-thousand exception, but we've not met him). And, increasingly, girls do also. Masturbation is similar for guys and girls—at least initially—in that it starts as exploration and curiosity. But after an initial experience or two, masturbation is a very different issue for guys than it is for girls.

We don't have space to go into massive detail here, so we'll offer a few compact thoughts: First, don't freak out. When your teenage guy says he wants to wash his own sheets, let him. If you happen to "catch him in the act" (Lord, please spare us all that), please take a lighthearted "well, that was awkward" approach.

Second, know that masturbation (particularly for guys) is a developmentally normal part of a changing body (and a culture that has a major gap between sexual readiness and marriage). Even conservative psychologist and family advocate James Dobson wrote, "It is my opinion that masturbation is not much of an issue with God. It's a normal part of adolescence, which involves no one else…if you do [masturbate], it is my opinion that you should not struggle with guilt over it."[20]

Third and finally, masturbation can easily become a destructive obsession (mostly for guys). When we write "easily" in that sentence, we're suggesting that a sizeable percentage of the teenage guys we know struggle with this. And it's almost exclusively linked to viewing Internet porn. We address this a little bit in the following section, but we could write an entire book on this alone—and in fact, one of us did. Please read another book in this series, co-authored by Marko and Adam McLane, called *A Parent's Guide to Understanding Social Media*, where protecting your teenager from these issues is addressed more fully.

Pornography

In 1 Corinthians 6, Paul exhorts the Corinthian church to "flee from sexual immorality." In the Greek, the word for "sexual immorality" is the word *porneia*. Look familiar? It's a general word for sexual sin, and it's used all over Scripture for different acts of sexual immorality. This covers more than just premarital sex; this is *anything* and *everything* your brain can think of that isn't what God intended.

Here's the difficult truth: Your teenager will be exposed to porn, if they haven't already. Around 93 percent of boys and 62 percent of girls are exposed to Internet pornography before the age of 18.[21] Instead of ignoring it or shaming your teen about it, graciously understand and engage in conversation about pornography. Talk with them about it, and address the heart issues of human sexuality and identity, not just the behaviors. Examine your own heart and lifestyle regarding pornography, not trying to pull out a speck in your teenager's eye before removing the plank from your own.

You can set up healthy boundaries now in order to help your teen. Installing filters and software on computers, tablets, smartphones, and any other device that can access the Internet can be incredibly helpful in both prevention and accountability. Keep computers in public areas of the house, and note whether your teenager is using the Internet late at night while the family sleeps.

Oral Sex

Just a quick note here: The majority of teenagers today do not consider oral sex to be sex. And this is particularly of note with Christian teenagers raised in a context where "don't have sex before marriage" is a message they've heard dozens, or hundreds, of times. Yup, talking about this is awkward—there's simply no way around. But *not* talking about it—what educators call a null curriculum—often communicates just as much as what we would say.

Treat the subject of oral sex just as you would any other topic in this book: with grace and normalization, anchoring it to our identities (the stuff in the first chapter of this book).

Homosexuality

The two of us went back and forth on how to write this section and what to say to you. The reality is that there's almost no more divisive subject in the church today. And if we're being completely honest with you, this subject has become *more* complex and nuanced for both of us over the years, not *less*. Some of that comes from our conversations with hundreds of teenagers struggling with their sexuality, tormented over same-sex attraction and the perceived implications for their faith and their relationships with family and church (including many who have walked away from the church because they were convinced it wasn't a safe place for honest dialogue).

Of course, there are dozens of helpful books on this topic alone. And although they are not written exclusively to parents, we would both highly recommend two books to you if your son or daughter is struggling with same-gender attraction (or if you suspect that they are): *Love Is an Orientation* by Andrew Marin (IVP, 2009), written to a general Christian audience and not specifically about teenagers; and *What Do I Do When Teenagers Question Their Sexuality?* by Steven Gerali (Zondervan, 2010), about teenagers, but written to youth workers.

This subject seems easy to have an opinion about until it's your own son or daughter who's wrestling with sexual identity. We'd like to give you three short pieces of advice:

- **Be ready with love.** Even if you have absolutely zero indication that your child might be struggling in this area, think through (and talk through, if there are two parents in your home) how you would respond if your child came out to you. Knowing that you'd intend to respond with love is absolutely essential. Every person, regardless of their sexuality, is created in the image of God and worthy of love and dignity and grace.

- **Grease the conversational rails.** Even if your child is as straight as straight can be, conversations about homosexuality and faith are not to be avoided. Make your home and relationship a safe place to talk, free from knee-jerk condemnation or pejorative remarks about anyone's sexuality. Continue to create a culture of honesty in your family, particularly with sensitive subjects like this one. You want to be the kind of parent that your children will run to for wisdom and grace, not run away from out of fear of misunderstanding or rejection.

- **Read more, learn more.** Particularly if you wonder about your teenager's sexuality, or if they've given you hints, pursue some intentional learning. Reach out to a gay Christian and listen—non-judgmentally—to his or her story. Read a book about faith and homosexuality that you don't expect you'll fully agree with. Understanding this issue beyond generalizations and simplistic doctrines will help you engage at a heart level. And it probably goes without saying that it's helpful to know the perspective of your faith community (particularly if your teenager is in a youth group).

Modesty and Clothing

Funny story: At the age of 16 years old, I (Joel) and my best friend, Brian, created a set of modesty rules for girls.

While on a mission trip to Mexico, we formed a list of mandates about what made a girl modest or not, and we were unafraid to share these mandates with our female mission teammates. This resulted in Brian literally being cornered by a crowd of angry young women who were quite frustrated with Brian's judgments on the length of their shorts. I was nowhere to be found during this incident.

Modesty is difficult to define, but we know it when we see it. Modesty doesn't mean striving to be unfashionable or frumpy. Nor does it mean a list of measurements for skirt length, tank-top straps, bare midriffs, or sagging pants. It certainly doesn't mean wearing only clothes purchased from Christian bookstores or bands.

In Chapter Three, we wrote about how guys *tend* to miss the *imago dei* in other, and girls *tend* to miss the *imago dei* in themselves. We see this show up so often in matters of clothing. When girls, in particular, dress in a revealing way, they often unknowingly (sometimes knowingly) create a continuous loop: Guys notice them (as objects) and girls are happy to be noticed (even as objects), so they dress as objects to be noticed, perpetuating the cycle.

Here's the bottom line: How we dress matters. How we clothe ourselves shapes the way we communicate and carry ourselves with others. If you show up to a job interview wearing gym clothes, it communicates. If a young woman wears a low-cut blouse and miniskirt, it communicates. If a young man walks around town shirtless, it communicates. Lauren Winner asks a fantastic question: "What stories do we want to tell ourselves and others through our choices of clothing?"[22] Clothes tell a story about who we are, what matters to us, and what we believe about ourselves and others.

Sexual Talk and Joking

Blunt reality #1: You would probably be shocked to hear how teenagers—particularly guys—talk about sexuality. It's just not the same as when you were that age, believe us.

Blunt reality #2: Unless you stoop as low as teenagers in this area (and you probably wouldn't be reading this book if that description fits you), you'll never hear this. This is an aspect of the underground world of today's teenagers that adults are *rarely* invited into.

But know this: How you talk and joke about sexual issues lays the groundwork for what your teenager will assume is OK. And they will rarely consider the reality that they and their friends take things 10 times, or a hundred times, further. The solution isn't avoiding talking about sex, or even avoiding joking! The solution is adhering to the truth of the *imago dei* in everyone when we talk or joke about sex. Talk about sex. Joke about sex! Just do so with a sense of reverence for the image of God in others.

Social Media

First, we want to once again point you to another book in this series that you need to read: *A Parent's Guide to Understanding Social Media*, by Marko and Adam McLane.

Clearly, the overwhelming presence of social media (online and mobile tools that host social interactions) has changed the very fabric of teenage relationships. Most adults leverage social media in utilitarian ways, to *supplement* our real-world relationships. But for teenagers today, there's no distinction between real world and online (or mobile). Texting, Facebook®, and other apps and tools don't merely supplement; they are usually part of the DNA of teenage relational webs.

As such, sexuality gets played out constantly in these online and mobile spaces as much as it does in real life—

sometimes (due to the perceived "safety" of online and mobile) even more so, with teenagers doing and saying more via text and Facebook than they ever would if they were face to face.

It's critical that you are engaged in this conversation *with* your teenager. Help them understand that nothing said online is truly private, and that anything can easily become public. Create boundaries for your entire household (that you also adhere to!) that help everyone disconnect and make wise choices. And we would say that it's fair for you as a parent to have access to your teenager's social media passwords (and cell phone) to occasionally check in.

Grace and Purity – Sexual Healing for Your Teen (and Yourself)

Scripture tells us to be pure, but no one's sexual history is spotless. We have all fallen short of the sexual ideal God has painted for us in his Word. But that doesn't mean we're failures.

Parents, you might have a messy sexual past. You might even be struggling with sexual sin right now. You need to know that God's grace is sufficient and that he promises to heal and make us pure through Christ. Confess your sin to Christ, and allow him to heal and restore.

We've all made mistakes. Your teenager will make mistakes, too. The question is, *will you respond with condemnation or compassion, with guilt trips or grace*? Our prayer is that this little book would open a door for you to start a conversation with your teen about sexuality and dating, that you and your teen would find both wholeness and holiness in your sexuality.

ENDNOTES

1. Sari Locker, *The Complete Idiot's Guide to Amazing Sex* (New York: Alpha Books, 2002), 9.

2. Lauren F. Winner, *Real Sex: The Naked Truth About Chastity* (Grand Rapids, MI: Brazos Press, 2005).

3. Rob Bell, *Sex God: Exploring the Endless Connections Between Sexuality and Spirituality* (Grand Rapids, MI: Zondervan, 2007), 53.

4. *Sexual Behavior, Sexual Attraction, and Sexual Identity in the United States: Data From the 2006-2008 National Survey of Family Growth*, National Health Statistics Reports, Number 36, March 3, 2011.

5. *Teenagers in the United States: Sexual Activity, Contraceptive Use, and Childbearing, 2006-2010 National Survey of Family Growth*, Vital and Health Statistics, Series 23, Number 31, October 2011.

6. Ibid.

7. Timothy Keller, *The Meaning of Marriage: Facing the Complexities of Commitment with the Wisdom of God* (New York: Dutton, 2011), 223.

8. givemesexjesus.com, last accessed October 22, 2012.

9. Winner, 33.

10. Winner, 89.

11. Keller, 208.

12. William M. Struthers, *Wired for Intimacy: How Pornography Hijacks the Male Brain* (Downers Grove, IL: InterVarsity Press, 2009), 85.

13. Keller, 205.

14. Benoit Denizet-Lewis, *Friends, Friends With Benefits and the Benefits of the Local Mall* (New York Times Magazine, May 30, 2004).

15. Derek Thompson, *The Death (and Life) of Marriage in America* (The Atlantic, February 7, 2012).

16. D'Vera Cohn, Jeffrey Passel, Wendy Wang, Gretchen Livingston, *Barely Half of U.S. Adults Are Married – A Record Low* (Pew Research Center, pewsocialtrends.org/2011/12/14/barely-half-of-u-s-adults-are-married-a-record-low, last accessed October 22, 2012).

17. Tyler Charles, *The Secret Sexual Revolution* (RelevantMagazine.com, February 20, 2012, relevantmagazine.com/life/relationship/features/28337-the-secret-sexual-revolution, last accessed October 22, 2012).

18. Winner, 126.

19. Ibid.

20. James Dobson, *Preparing for Adolescence* (Ventura, CA: Regal, 1989), 83-84.

21. Walt Mueller, *A Parent's Primer on Internet Pornography* (CPYU, digitalkidsinitiative.com/files/2012/07/Parent_Primer_Internet_Pornography1.pdf, last accessed October 22, 2012).

22. Winner, 77.

Check out the NEW
PARENT'S GUIDE website!

Check out all the books in our *PARENT'S GUIDE* Series!

A Parent's Guide to Understanding **Teenage Guys**
A Parent's Guide to Understanding **Teenage Girls**
A Parent's Guide to Understanding **Sex & Dating**
A Parent's Guide to Understanding **Teenage Brains**
A Parent's Guide to Understanding **Social Media**

Visit **SimplyYouthMinistry.com** to learn more about each of these books!